"I only popped out for som
and what happened next has co....,.....,.......,....
my life."

"They just offered to pray for me. No-one has ever done that before. It really helped me."

"I was blind drunk leaving the night club. They were unpaid volunteers who took care of me without asking for anything in return."

"I went with a friend for a coffee and there was some sort of meeting going on in the coffee shop. Someone was talking about how God had changed their life. I'm not religious, but what was said connected with me..."

"I had noticed them a few times on the street offering to pray with people, but never gave it a second thought. Then something terrible happened in my family. I needed someone to help and found myself saying "yes" to their prayers."

What's going on?

Something unusual is happening on our streets. Christians are getting out of their church buildings to meet complete strangers in pubs, coffee shops and on the street.

They come from every type of church background and none of them are asking for money. In fact, they are not asking for anything. Instead, they are offering to chat, listen and pray for the people they bump into.

What God has given them they want to share with others. They are becoming pro-active. The church building is no longer recognised as the only place where they can share their faith.

Instead, they are inviting friends and even complete strangers to meetings in cafes and pubs. They are getting out on the streets and into the market places, offering friendship, a listening ear and their prayers to those they speak to.

"Oh, I get it! The churches are losing numbers and getting empty and the ones left are feeling desperate. It's just a crafty way of trying to fill up the churches again, isn't it?"

Actually, very few conversations on the street are really about joining a church. Christians out there are not motivated by desperation but inspiration. It is what the Lord has done in their lives that motivates them to speak to and care for complete strangers on the street - at all times of the day and night.

"Well that's OK for them and I'm sure religion is helping them. But I've never been religious and never seen the point of it."

" 'Religious' is probably the last word they would use to describe themselves. What they all have in common is not religion but a real relationship with the God who made the whole universe and everything in it."

"You've lost me now. What do you mean by 'relationship' with God?"

We believe God came to this earth and lived among us - not as a spirit or ghost, but as a real flesh and blood human being. This was Jesus.

"I've heard a little bit about Jesus Christ. He went about doing good. No-one really knocks him, but he tragically finished up being crucified."

That's right. But if he really was God in human form he needn't have gone through all that suffering. He could have avoided it.

"So why should we take this idea seriously, that he was God in human form, when he finished up on a cross?"

Many people know about the crucifixion, but fewer know what happened next...

Three days after he was buried he reappeared in a new supernatural but physical body. He hadn't been resuscitated. He was buried with soldiers guarding his tomb from Friday afternoon to Sunday morning. It's impossible to resuscitate a body that's been dead that long.

"So what you are saying is that he came back as some sort of ghost. It's not all that unusual. I hear stories like that all the time."

It didn't happen like that. His new body was very special. It was physical and had the wounds of his crucifixion on it. But it wasn't his old body. It was different. Some of his friends at first thought he was a ghost. But once they touched his flesh and had meals with him they knew that was impossible.

Jesus proved he was God, not by dying on a cross, but by being raised supernaturally from the dead. His enemies tried desperately to find his corpse, but it no longer existed.

He still has that body. Christians know he is alive because they have a personal relationship with him.

"Well, that all sounds very fascinating, but it's really nothing to do with me. It's really none of my business!"

In fact, it is. Let me explain it like this. Jesus, the Son of God, chose to die on the cross. He didn't have to suffer, but he chose to go through all that. He lived a perfect life. He never put a foot wrong. He never deserved to suffer at all. But he chose to do that, not for himself, but for us.

"Now this really is getting serious. But I don't like the idea of a God who punishes people and makes them suffer. I thought your God was a God of love."

He is. But just think about a world in which wrongdoing is never punished: a world in which evil people get away with their crimes. Could a loving God really allow such a world like that. A world with no punishment for wrongdoing is a world without justice. God is not just loving, he is also just.

"God made Jesus who had no sin to be sin for us, so that we might become right before God."

"Ok. I get that. But why does God have to punish people. Why not let them off?"

Because he is a holy God. "Holiness" means living without any blemish or stain on one's life: in effect, living a perfect life. Only Jesus has ever lived such a life on earth. No-one could ever find any fault in him - they still can't. But this is how much Jesus loves each one of us. He was willing to suffer the punishment that we deserve. That's what we mean when we say that "he died for us". He did it so that God may accept each one of us as perfect.

When we clean the car, the dirt on the car comes onto the cloth. The clean cloth becomes dirty so that the car can become clean. In the same way, Jesus took our dirt on himself and suffered for it, so that we might become perfectly clean.

"So Jesus died for everybody and as a result, everybody goes to heaven."

Not really. If heaven was automatic, we could all do what we wanted in this life and get away with it.

"Just a minute. If Jesus died to take God's punishment from us and onto himself and make us fit for heaven; and if he did that for everybody, then how come not everyone goes to heaven? I don't get that."

It does sound like a bit of a contradiction doesn't it? Actually the key to sorting this confusion can be found in a single verse in the Bible:

"If you confess with your mouth, "Jesus is Lord," and believe in your heart that God raised him from the dead, you will be saved. For it is with your heart that you believe and are made right with God, and it is with your mouth that you are saved." *(Romans 10:9,10)*

"So that means that as long as we believe what you've told us we'll be OK. Is that it?"

Not quite. Let me explain...

The key words in this passage are: "believe in your heart." This means far more than just accepting what others believe.

"Now you've lost me..."

Let me put it like this. Suppose you walk into a room and see someone that you immediately fall in love with. You believe in your heart this is the person that one day you will marry. Imagine how you would feel. It would be far more than just a casual thought like "he or she's the one!" What you believe in your heart would affect everything. You would want to meet this person, get to know this person, be with this person as much as possible and tell all your friends about this person.

What you *believe* in your heart affects your thinking, your emotions and your lifestyle - in fact, it affects everything!

It's the same with Jesus. When we truly believe in our hearts that he died for us, it changes what we think about everything. Our entire life changes.

"So how do I believe in my heart?"

When we fall in love, that person becomes a part of our heart. They are not just an acquaintance, like our friends at work: we have a heart relationship.

Similarly, when we believe in our hearts what Jesus has done for us, we begin a heart relationship with him. Because he continues to have a human body, we have connection with him. He is able to come and dwell in our human hearts, but he only does this if we are willing to invite him in. Our relationship with him begins when we invite him in.

"How do I do that?"

Just talk to him. Use your own words. He hears everything you say. Tell him how you feel. Be honest with him. If you now realise for the first time that he died for you, thank him for that. Tell him you want to turn away from what's wrong in your life. Then take a step of faith and ask him to come into your heart, to be your saviour and friend forever.

"I'm finding this really difficult. Can you help me?"

Here's a simple prayer of faith you can use. But there's nothing magic about the words. They need to express what is real in your heart, so make them your own.

"Lord Jesus Christ, I really do believe you died on the cross to wash away my wrongdoing and to make me completely clean. I turn my back on everything in my life that offends you and ask you to come into my heart and life and be my saviour and friend forever. Amen."

Jesus makes the following promise in the Bible:

"I stand at the door (of your hearts) and knock. If anyone hears my voice and opens the door, I will come in and eat with him, and him with me."
(Revelation 3:20)

He always keeps his promises.

"So what happens now?"

God has a special and unique purpose and plan for your life, but it takes time for these things to unfold. He wants to reveal himself to you more and more.

Usually the best way forward is to begin to meet with other Christians - especially when they meet informally in their homes. Getting to know a few Christians will give you the help and encouragement that you need as a new Christian. You'll probably have loads of questions, and they'll be able to help.

You may know some Christians already. If not, use the contact details on the back of this booklet of someone who will be able to help you. You could also make contact with the vicar or minister or pastor of a local church by checking their details on the net.